MINI COLOR SERIES

7512

Rolling Steel

NATO's Self-Propelled Guns

Text & Photos by Carl Schulze & Walter Böhm
Edited by James R. Hill
Illustrations by Hubert Cance

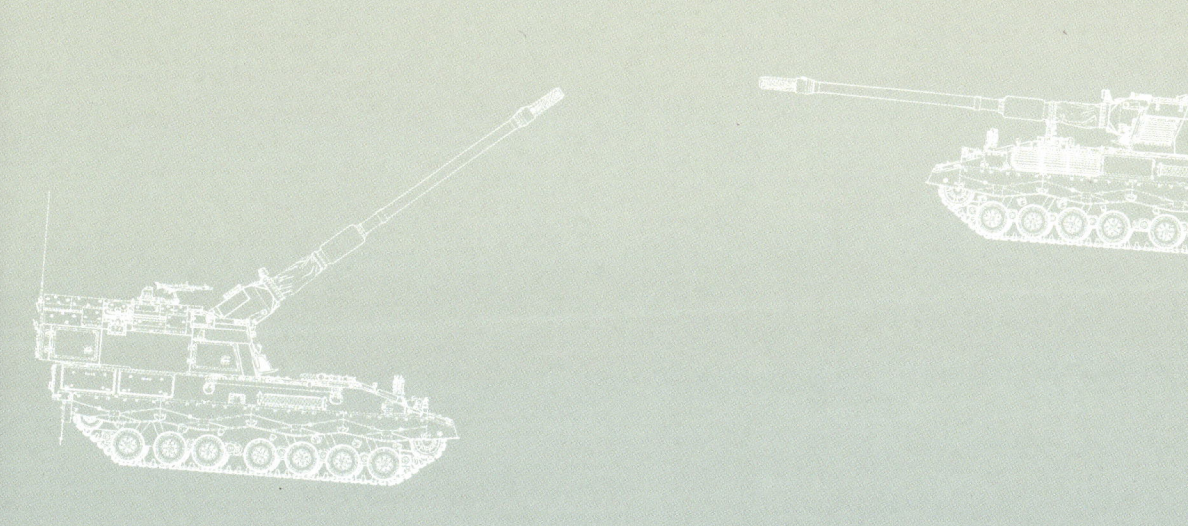
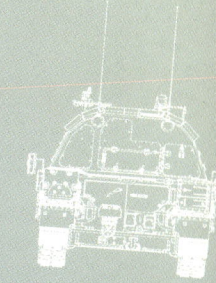
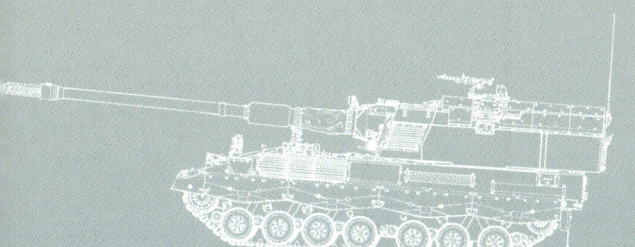
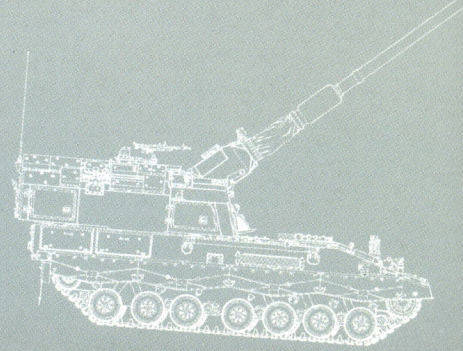

Editor: James R. Hill

Copyright © 2004

by CONCORD PUBLICATIONS CO.

603-609 Castle Peak Road

Kong Nam Industrial Building

10/F, B1, Tsuen Wan

New Territories, Hong Kong

www.concord-publications.com

We welcome authors who can help
expand our range of books. If you
would like to submit material,
please feel free to contact us.

We are always on the look-out for new,
unpublished photos for this series.
If you have photos or slides or
information you feel may be useful to
future volumes, please send them to us
for possible future publication.
Full photo credits will be given upon
publication.

ISBN 962-361-679-1

printed in Hong Kong

Introduction

NATO's conception of warfare – combined arms fighting on the battlefield – is marked by the combination and cooperation of the firepower and mobility of battalion-, brigade-, and division-scale units. Another factor is the capability to destroy the mobility of hostile forces by barrage and obstacles. Modern mechanized infantry and armored units are dependent on artillery protection. Self-propelled guns are an important element of this concept.

Modern artillery weapon systems, such as the British AS 90, the French GCT AUF-1, the American M109A6 Paladin, and the German Panzerhaubitze PzH 2000 have multi-role requirements – fire support against hostile elements on the frontline, ahead of their own combat units, and fire against hostile follow-on forces and artillery positions – and hostile control, support and air-defense positions have become targets for today's modern artillery systems.

Today, modern weapon systems like the AS 90, AUF-1, M109A6, and PzH 2000 fire ordnance with increased ranges up to 40 kilometers (25 miles). This allows the self-propelled guns to send their shells deep into hostile territory to reduce the threat to their own fighting elements.

Panzerhaubitze PzH 2000

The first steps for research and development of the PzH 2000 can be traced back to November 1987. In 1986, Italy, Great Britain and Germany canceled their cooperation on the SP-70 self-propelled howitzer program. Great Britain developed the AS 90 howitzer and introduced this weapon system to the British Army units. The German government decided to develop a front-driven 155mm howitzer as a replacement for the aged M109A3GE self-propelled howitzer. The M109A3GE was a German improvement of the US M109A2/A3 series, but the general design represented the standards of the decade between 1960 and 1970.

Development and Characteristics

After the tri-national SP-70 program was canceled in 1986, the German government awarded the contract for the development and construction of a new 155mm self-propelled howitzer weapon system to two German consortia. The first consortium was Gruppe Nord with the firms Wegmann and MaK; the second consortium was Gruppe Süd with Krauss-Maffei, Rheinmetall and KUKA. Based on the Bundeswehr requirements and tactical efforts, a new program called "Panzerhaubitze 2000" was founded in 1987. The Nord consortium developed a trial vehicle called the "PT 02," which was based on the proven Leopard 1 MBT chassis. The Süd consortium developed the "PT 01" prototype, which was based on elements of the Leopard 2 chassis.

In 1990, these two vehicles were intensively tested, and the "PT 02" was the winner of the competition. The German government selected the vehicle and placed orders to Wegmann/MaK for four identical trial vehicles. These vehicles were built and modified permanently according to Bundeswehr requirements between 1991 and 1993. In the early 1990s, the concept of a vehicle and weapon system with ordnance and electronic equipment was a significant advantage and a technological leap into the 21st century.

The emblem of the Bundeswehr's Artillerieschule *at Rilchenberg Kaserne in Idar- Oberstein. This emblem is affixed to the front of the hull of a PzH 2000. (Walter Böhm)*

The main requests for capabilities in the new PzH 2000 were as follows:
- maximum range up to 30 kilometers (19 miles) using the standard NATO 155mm projectile
- 60 projectiles in "on board" storage
- automatic guiding of the main gun
- automatic loading mechanis
- reduction of the crew to five soldiers
- NBC protection for the crew compartment and ammunition storage
- independent vehicle navigation system
- independent operation on the battlefield supported by a vehicle's own ballistic fire control computer.

The PzH 2000 needs only 30 seconds from movement to readiness for fire. After a fire order is received, eight rounds can be fired in one minute. The first three rounds leave the gun within 10 seconds. The procedure to prepare the vehicle for a change of position requires less than 30 seconds. A well-trained crew needs only two minutes total from driving to preparation for fire, fire, and leaving the position. This quick movement makes it very difficult for hostile artillery radar or forward observers to discover the PzH 2000 positions.

In 1994, intensive testing and troop trials took place in Germany and in foreign countries. Only one year later the PzH 2000 was ready for introduction. In March 1996, Wegmann was awarded the order for an initial batch of 185 PzH 2000 vehicles. In mid-1998, the first vehicles were delivered to the German Bundeswehr. The last vehicles of the first batch were handed over to Bundeswehr units in 2002. Due to the high price and the reduced number of systems, only the Bundeswehr KRK units and some few HVK units received the Panzerhaubitze 2000. The first 185 systems were issued to the *Artillerieschule* (School of Artillery) based in Idar Oberstein; *Panzerartillerielehrbatallion* 345 based in Kusel; PzArtLBtl 95 based in Munster; PzArtBtl 405 based in Dabel; and PzArtBtl 115 based in Neunburg v. Wald.

In 1998, the Panzerartilleriebataillonen *of the German Bundeswehr received their first PzH 2000s. A total of 185 Panzerhaubitze 2000 will replace the aged M109A3GE. The first PzH 2000 vehicles were delivered to the* Artillerieschule *based in Idar-Oberstein for troop training. Notice the difference in size between the huge PzH 2000 and the M109A3GE. The PzH 2000 should be in Bundeswehr inventory for decades to come. This new weapon system has become the backbone of the artillery fire support in the German Army. Some of the German M109A3GE will receive a last upgrade to the M109A3GEA2 standard, which will make them usable for few more years. (Walter Böhm)*

This PzH 2000 of the Artillerieschule *at Idar-Oberstein is fitted with a special gunfire simulator that allows fire missions to be simulated without driving to the range. The crew members of the new PzH 2000 were trained at the* Artillerieschule. *The* Gruppe Weiterentwicklung *(Section Development), as a part of the* Artillerieschule, *is working continuously on upgrade and research programs for the German Bundeswehr's* Artillerietruppe. *(Walter Böhm)*

The vehicles of the first batch of PzH 2000 were delivered to the Artillerieschule, *HVK* Verbände *(German Bundeswehr main defense forces)* and *KRK* Verbände *(German Bundeswehr crisis reaction forces)*. As the first regular unit, Panzerartillerielehrbataillon 345 *(PzArtLBtl 345)*, which is based in Kusel, received their first PzH 2000 in 1999. The markings on the hull of this PzH 2000 are, from left to right: Military Load Class (MLC), Bundeswehr vehicle registration number, and tactical sign of 2nd Lehrbatterie, *PzArtLBtl 345*. (Walter Böhm)

One of the main requirements for the new German howitzer was an increased range of fire. There are only two possible ways to increase the range of a weapon when the caliber is standardized: rocket-assisted projectiles or a longer gun barrel. The Bundeswehr decided on the latter option. Now the PzH 2000 rifled 155mm L52 ordnance is 8 meters (26 feet) long. (Walter Böhm)

Turret, Ordnance and Ammunition

The main armament of the PzH 2000 is the Rheinmetall-built, 52-caliber (8-meter [26-ft]) long, rifled 155mm L52 howitzer. Its chrome plated barrel provides the main gun with a long-wearing life. The gun barrel is fitted with a slot-type muzzle brake and a bore evacuator. The gun can also be used in a direct firefight. The turret can traverse a complete 360 degrees, and firing is possible in all turret positions. The maximum elevation of the gun is up to + 65 degrees. Using the *Modulares Treibladungssystem* (MTLS), the gun's range is up to 30 km (19 miles) with the standard L15A2 projectile and up to 40 km (25 miles) with extended range ammunition. For anti-aircraft and defense purposes, a 7.62mm Fla MG3 is mounted in front of the left hatch on the roof of the turret. Eight smoke dischargers are located on the front of the turret near the main gun.

The huge turret is made of armored steel plates and designed in accordance with the shape of European railway tunnels. The inside of the turret and hull is covered with a liner to protect against artillery fragments. The charge storage area is separate from the crew compartment in the rear of the turret. Main electronic systems like the fire control system and the gun control system with the added tracking and observing systems are located in the turret.

The commander has at his disposal the PERI-R19 periscope, a PERI-RTNL80 traversable periscope with laser rangefinder and passive night sights. The gunner uses the *Panzerzielfernrohr* PzFTN80, the vehicle navigation system and the MICMOC ballistic fire control computer for calculating the fire orders. On the roof of the turret there are mounts to fit additional reactive armor elements. The crew can quickly attach these elements using only the vehicle's own tools. These reactive armor elements protect against bomblet ammunition, but they are mounted only in the event of war.

Hull and Chassis

The PzH 2000 is front driven and has a torsion-bar suspension chassis. Seven double-tired roadwheels, four track-return rollers, the drive sprocket on the front, and the idler at the rear on each side complete the chassis. Some components were based on the well-proven Leopard 1 and 2 MBT. The hull is of welded construction using armored steel plates in different dimensions. The engine compartment is separated from the crew compartment by a fire wall. The powerpack is a combination of the MTU MT881 Ka-500 engine with 1005 PS (736KW) and the Renk HSWL 284C transmission. The 55-ton PzH 2000 has a maximum road speed of 60 km/h (37 mph).

The driver is located in the front of the hull right beneath the engine. Behind the engine is located the 60-round magazine with the automatic loader. The PzH 2000 has a fuel storage capacity of up to 1000 liters (264 gallons) of diesel fuel, which gives the vehicle a range of 420 km (261 miles) in good conditions.

Summary

The PzH 2000 became the standard self-propelled howitzer for the German Bundeswehr's *Kriesenreaktionskräfte* (KRK), or crisis reaction force. The enormous growth potential, the advanced technologies and the new conception give the PzH 2000 the capability to fulfill all requirements of an up-to-date artillery weapon system. The PzH 2000 is ready for all challenges on the future digitalized and three-dimensional battlefield.

In international use, the PzH 2000 is in first place; more and more it has become a standard artillery system of the European forces. In July 2001, Greece ordered 24 PzH 2000 from Wegmann. The armies of both the Netherlands and Italy decided to introduce the PzH 2000 into their artillery units. In October 2001, Sweden began testing the PzH 2000 in a coastal defense role and for their army's artillery.

The combination of the new L52 gun barrel and the Modulares Treibladungssystem (MTLS modular charge system) increased the range from 30 kilometers (19 miles) with the L15A2 standard projectile up to 40 kilometers (25 miles) using extended range ammunition. The red and white over-wide alert panels were opened during road marches on civil roads. (Walter Böhm)

The weapon is a combination of the L52 ordnance with the slot-type muzzle break fitted to the breechblock, the recoil and recuperator system, a temperature sensor for the thermal data management, and an elevation mechanism interface. (Walter Böhm)

In contrast to the welded aluminum construction of the M109A6 Paladin, the PzH 2000 is made with steel plates. The huge turret has a storage area in the rear for the extremely flammable and explosive charges that is completely separate from the crew compartment. (Walter Böhm)

The vehicle commander is located behind the PERI-RTNL 80, and loader 1 (Ladekanonier 1) is positioned beside him. Loader 1 is responsible for the MG3 7.62mm anti-aircraft machine gun. Separated from the other crew members, the driver is located in the right front of the hull. (Walter Böhm)

The huge turret of the PzH 2000 is positioned very low in relation to the rear of the hull. This reduces the projection of the gun barrel and allows the crew to enter the vehicle through the rear door. (Walter Böhm)

A PzH 2000 of 2.Batterie, PzArtLBtl 345 takes up a position in the assembly area during Exercise "Westpfalz" in January 2000. The howitzer is positioned under the trees and covered with camouflage nets to hide it from aircraft. The Ladekanonier (loader) guards the vehicle with the anti-aircraft machine gun. (Walter Böhm)

After the introduction of the PzH 2000 into the Bundeswehr artillery units, the aged M113A2 G OPTRONIC used for forward observation will be replaced by an upgraded and modified Leopard 1A5 MBT. With the intended introduction of the modified Leopard 1A5 for the forward observer role, the forward observers will have the same mobility by night and day as other modern mechanized units. This will be combined with much better armor protection, in contrast to the light armored aluminum-built M113A2 G OPTRONIC. The target screening capability is the same as the old M113-based observer vehicle, but in the new Leopard 1A5-based forward observer vehicle, the crew can control a greater variety of fire missions. By 1999 two trial vehicles were built. The Beobachtungspanzer Artillierie Leopard (BeopPzArtLeop) shown here carries the tactical markings of 4.L/PzArtLBtl 345. It was photographed during troop trials during a Bundeswehr exercise at CMTC Hohenfels. (Walter Böhm)

Insignia of 3.Batterie, Panzerartilleriebatallion 405. (Walter Böhm)

PzArtBtl 405, which belongs to the Bundeswehr's KRK units, is based in Dabel, Germany. PzArtBtl 405 is under order of PzGrenBrig 40 "Mecklenburg." The 3200 soldiers of PzGren Brigade 40 were located in different towns in Mecklenburg-Vorpommern (the former German Democratic Republic) and Niedersachsen (West Germany). Thus, PzGren Brigade 40 is a symbol of the Armee der deutschen Einheit (army of unified Germany). (Walter Böhm)

The PzH 2000 powerpack is a combination of the Typ 881 engine built by MTU and the HSWL transmission built by Renk. The MTU MT 881 Ka-500 engine is a development based on the proven 837 series engine (Leopard 1 MBT engine) and 873 series engine (Leopard 2 MBT engine). (Walter Böhm)

The powerpack of a PzH 2000 is lifted out after all the connectors between the Renk transmission and the drive sprockets have been unfastened. These connectors are fitted with a moveable sleeve to make it easier to remove. The powerpack is placed on the front of the hull beside the driver's position. (Walter Böhm)

A Bergepanzer 3 Büffel of PzBtl 84 lifts out the complete PzH 2000 powerpack using its 30-ton-capacity turnable crane. As of 2002, artillery units equipped the PzH 2000 still had the lighter Bergepanzer 2 Standard in their inventory. In the near future these units will re-equip with the more powerful Bergepanzer 3 Büffel. (Walter Böhm)

Details of the PzH 2000's turret. The turret's roof is fitted with an anti-slip surface. The screw mounts can be used to affix additional reactive armor elements to provide better protection for the crew and ammunition. (Walter Böhm)

The L52 gun's barrel is chrome plated to extend its life. The 155mm L52 ordnance of the PzH 2000 can be used in both towed and self-propelled howitzers. The barrel is connected to the breechblock by an interrupted thread, which makes it possible to quickly remove the barrel from the outside without dismantling the whole weapon system. (Walter Böhm)

Ammunition ready for use. To give the PzH 2000 a high tactical availability on the battleground, the howitzer has racks for 60 155mm projectiles and the corresponding 288 MTLS (Modulares Treibladungs System) charges stored in an automatically operating magazine. Ammunition for the 7.62mm anti-aircraft machine gun, spare smoke grenade charges, and ammunition for the crew's weapons complete the inventory of stored ammunition. (Walter Böhm)

Close-up photo of the PzH 2000's gun travel lock. The hydraulically operated gun travel lock can fasten and unfasten by remote control under armor protection of the turret. While the vehicle is traveling, the barrel is fixed in the 12 o'clock position. The rectangular plate on the gun's front end is part of the muzzle velocity measuring system. (Walter Böhm)

155mm smoke/fog projectiles for use with the PzH 2000. At the time of this writing a special smoke/fog grenade was under development. The so-called Multispektral-Nebel-Granate has the ability to disturb optical observation, as well as radio, infrared or short wave sensors. (Walter Böhm)

Today the MAN 10tgl 8x8 truck used for transporting ammunition to the PzH 2000. Fitted with a small loading crane, the MAN 10tgl has an empty weight of 15.4 tons and a loading capacity up to 10 tons. In the future, the PzH 2000 units will be issued the new heavy MAN 15tgl 8x8 MULTI truck as the standard ammunition carrier. (Walter Böhm)

The automatic electrically driven projectile-loading system allows for loading and firing in every turret position. The ordnance can be loaded no matter what the turret traverse or gun elevation. The magazine is constructed to keep all of the 60 projectiles on board. (Walter Böhm)

In case of a malfunction of the fully automatic loader and magazine systems, all operations can be performed manually by the crew's two loaders. Under normal conditions, when all systems are operable, the crew can rearm all 60 of the projectiles and charges in less than 12 minutes. This leaves the two loaders with only one job: to put the projectiles on the endless conveyor so they can be automatically transported into the magazine. If a vehicle should suffer a breakdown, the magazine can be unloaded the same way. (Walter Böhm)

Here a PzH 2000 deploys to a firing position area (FSR-Feuerstellungsraum) at the training area at Klietz, near Berlin, Germany. The FSR for a Panzerartilleriebatterie (howitzer battery) can be as vast as three square kilometers. This FSR is normally located 8-10 kilometers (5-6 miles) behind the so-called VRV-Vorderer Rand der Verteidigung (line of defense). In the FSR there are various fire positions for the two Panzerartilleriezug (two howitzer platoons). (Walter Böhm)

The PzH 2000 can fire when the ordnance has an elevation from –2.5 degrees up to +65 degrees. Loading and firing can occur independently of the positioning of the turret. From moving to firing, a well-trained crew requires only 30 seconds. (Walter Böhm)

Panzerhaubitze 2000, 2nd Company, *Panzerartillerielehrbataillon* 345, Baumholder ranges 2002

Panzerhaubitze 2000 of 2nd Company, *Panzerartillerielehrbataillon* 345 seen during the "System Artillerie" demonstration on the Baumholder ranges in autumn 2002. The red flag mounted on the turret indicates that the gun is loaded and ready to fire. Only markings visible is the German national identification sign, an iron cross on the turret side. The gun is painted in the standard NATO three color camouflage pattern.

"Firepower." The PzH 2000 operates in the FSR on the platoon level with three howitzers. When the guns receive the order for a fire mission, they leave their assembly areas and attack the hostile targets depending on the intentions of the Brigadeartillerieführer *(leader of artillery units supporting a brigade). (Walter Böhm)*

The PzH 2000 howitzer can fire eight projectiles a mere 30 seconds after it reaches the firing position, the first three rounds in less than 10 seconds. One possible scenario for a PzH 2000 platoon is to pin down hostile forces with their fire to give their own mechanized units time to rearrange and counterattack. (Walter Böhm)

After one minute of firing, the PzH 2000 will shift its position; preparation for this change of position takes only 30 seconds. Then, only two minutes after the PzH 2000 has stopped, the howitzer leaves the position. This quick, flexible operation on the battlefield is the best protection against hostile observation, reconnaissance and counterattack. (Walter Böhm)

After a day on the training range, the crew has to clean the L52 gun barrel in the usual fashion. The PzH 2000 has a crew of five: commander, driver, gunner, loader 1, and loader 2. In contrast to the aged M109A3GE with its crew of eight soldiers, the up-to-date equipment of the PzH 2000 does a better job with a reduced crew. (Walter Böhm)

Following the exercise, the howitzers are cleaned of mud and dust. The Technische Dienst (periodical technical check of all main vehicle and weapon systems) became necessary before the vehicles were loaded onto railway freight cars for the return to the unit's base. The PzH 2000 chassis has some elements of the Leopard 1 and 2 MBT. Four return rollers stabilize the tracks. (Walter Böhm)

Elements of 3.Batterie, PzArtBtl 405 travel on railway carriages near Klietz. The inside of the turret and hull of the PzH 2000 is covered by a liner that protects against small arms fire and artillery fragments. The huge turret is designed in accordance with the shape of European railway tunnels, which means the PzH 2000 can be transported without complications on all European main railway networks. (Walter Böhm)

The units of Panzerartilleriebataillon 2 belonged to Blauland (Blue Force) during "Hessischer Löwe 2002." They provided fire support for the blue elements during defensive and attack operations. During the Kampf mit dem Feuer battle tactics, the Blue Force's artillery elements were used for firing on Rotland (Red Force) artillery and troop concentrations deep in hostile territory. (Walter Böhm)

Emblem of PzArtBtl 405.

Panzerartilleriebataillon 2 received the first PzH 2000 vehicles in mid-2001. The PzArtBtl 2, which is under order of Panzergrenadierbrigade 14, participated with two fully equipped batteries in the Brigaderahmenübung (CFX) "Hessischer Löwe 2002." This exercise was held in January 2002 in the area around Göttingen, Einbeck Paderborn and Warburg. (Walter Böhm)

The German Bundeswehr's Panzerartilleriebataillonen of the KRK and the HVK were structured as follows after being equipped with the PzH 2000 weapon system: a Stabs und Versorgungskompanie (Headquarters and Support Company) and three Schießende Batterien (firing batteries), each with six PzH 2000 howitzers. The firing batteries are separated into two platoons, each with three guns, four forward observer troops with the M113A2 G BeobPzArt (Rohr), and one artillery observer radar group with M113A2ABRA Gefechtsfeldbeobachtungsradar (battlefield surveillance radar). (Walter Böhm)

AS 90 – Britain's Self-Propelled Howitzer

In 1993, the 1st Regiment Royal Horse Artillery was the first unit of the British Army to receive the new AS 90 Self-Propelled Howitzer. Since the time the AS 90 entered service with the British Army, it has replaced the entire fleet of older systems, namely the 155mm M109 and the 105mm Abbot. Today, the AS 90 is the only tracked self-propelled howitzer in the British Army's inventory.

Development History

Development of the AS 90 began as a private venture in the late 1970s. It came about during the production of the FH 70 155mm towed howitzer when Vickers Shipbuilding and Engineering Limited (VSEL, later Marconi Marine, Land and Naval Systems, which today belongs to BAE Systems RO Defence) discovered a need among the world's armed forces for new self-propelled artillery systems. This resulted in the GBT 155 turret, which used as its weapon system the FH 70 155mm ordnance, which was developed by Germany, Italy and Great Britain. The turret was designed to be mounted on various existing main battle tank chassis, such as on the T-72, and therefore be a cheap option for countries with a small defense budget seeking a modern artillery system. In 1982, the GBT turret was revealed to the public for the first time.

Using the GBT turret with a modified larger turret ring, VSEL conducted follow-on studies that led to the design of the AS 90. In March 1985, the project definition for the AS 90 reached its final status, and the first prototype was shown at the British Army Equipment Exhibition (BAEE) in June 1986. That same year the United Kingdom withdrew from the international 155mm SP 70 project, which presented the British Army with the need for a new option for the requested new artillery system in order to replace the 155mm M109 and the 105mm Abbot. Shortly after the BAEE, the British Army began extensive trials that resulted in the Live Crew Clearance Certification of the Ordnance Board for the AS 90 in 1987.

Between March and June 1987, during another package of extensive trials, the AS 90 traveled over 3000km (1863 miles) and fired approximately 1500 rounds without a major failure. In June 1988, the British Army selected the AS 90 and awarded a contract to VSEL for 300 million GBP for 179 AS 90s. Between 1989 and 1991, the Royal School of Artillery conducted additional reliability-and-growth trials during which the two existing prototypes traveled over 28,000km (17,388 miles) and fired more than 6100 rounds. In May 1992, the AS 90 was officially accepted for service in the British Army. By late 1992, the first production vehicles were delivered to the 1st Regiment Royal Horse Artillery, which

Rear view of an AS 90 of the 1st Regiment Royal Horse Artillery that was seen in the summer of 1993. The NBC and air conditioning systems are clearly visible on the rear of the turret. The three large storage boxes on the side are for storing the crewmembers' belongings, and another two are situated on the left side of the turret so each crewmember can use one exclusively. (Carl Schulze)

In 1993, the 1st Regiment Royal Horse Artillery was the first artillery unit of the British Army to reach operational status with the AS 90 self-propelled howitzer. Here AS 90s belonging to the regiment race into position during an exercise on the Salisbury Plain that same year. Fitted with the Autonomous navigation and Gun Laying System (AGLS), the AS 90 can operate independently of external sighting references, so gun positions need not to be prepared before the guns move in. (Carl Schulze)

During a demonstration an AS 90 of A Battery (The Chestnut Troop) of the 1st Regiment Royal Horse Artillery demonstrates the capability of firing a three-round burst in under ten seconds. A pair of AS 90s has the ability to deliver a payload of 261kg (576 lb) of HE ammunition on a single target at a distance of up to 24.7km (15 miles) in under ten seconds. Other rates of fire are:
- Intensive fire: Firing six rounds per minute for up to three minutes.
- Sustained fire: Firing two rounds a minute for a longer period.
Note the black stripe in front of the muzzle; it is the round just leaving the gun. (Carl Schulze)

by the summer of 1993 was the first operational AS 90 artillery regiment in the British Army.

Eight AS 90s, one of which was fitted with a Royal Ordnance Nottingham 155mm 52-caliber barrel, underwent a five-week In Service Reliability Demonstration (ISRD) in 1994. ISRD simulated a period of 80 battlefield days in which all guns together traveled 6000km (3726 miles) and fired a total of 11,2000 rounds. During these trials, the 52-caliber barrel proved its reliability and enhancement for the future.

In 1995, the last AS 90 left the manufacturer's plant at Barrow-in-Furness, Cumbria and was handed over to the British Army, while a couple of AS 90s remained with Marconi Marine, Land and Naval Systems for further trials. Since its introduction, the AS 90 Self-Propelled Howitzer has not taken part in a major conflict. However, AS 90 batteries of the Royal Artillery have been deployed in support of the British Army with IFOR/SFOR in Bosnia since 1995 and with KFOR in Kosovo since 1999. In addition, AS 90s saw action during various exercises in Canada, Poland, Germany, and Oman.

Vehicle Description

The AS 90 is a fully tracked, self-propelled howitzer that the British Army uses in the Divisional Close Artillery Support role. The crew consists of the driver, commander (No. 1), a gun layer (No. 3), and two loaders (No. 2 and No. 4). Usually one or two additional gunners are added to the crew in order to ensure that enough ammunition is ready during fire missions. The hull and turret of the AS 90 are constructed from all-welded

steel armor that can withstand the impact of infantry weapons' fire of up to 14.5mm and shell fragments from 152mm artillery shells.

The powerpack is situated at the front right of the chassis, and the driver, who directs the vehicle by means of a steering wheel, is positioned at the front left. The powerpack consists of the Cummins VTA 903T 660 90-degree, V8, four-stroke, liquid-cooled, diesel engine coupled with the ZF LSG 2000 fully automatic transmission, which offers four forward and two reverse gears. Close to the main engine is a diesel-powered auxiliary unit that allows the turret systems to operate and conduct fire missions without running the main engine.

The fighting compartment is situated behind the engine compartment in the rear of the vehicle. It can be entered through the large one-piece rear door that is also used for ammunition resupply. The turret is mounted above the fighting compartment on a turret ring that has a 2.7-meter (9-foot) diameter. The AS 90's running gear consists of six road wheels on either side of the chassis with an idler at the rear and a drive sprocket at the front. A high degree of cross-country capability is available through the use of a hydropneumatic suspension. The vehicle is fitted with a Dhiel double pin track.

The layer is seated to the right in the front of the turret, with the commander seated behind him. The loaders are positioned on the left hand side. The commander has a cupola above his position, and an air sentry hatch is situated on the left side of the turret roof. Next to this a 7.62mm GPMG is mounted on a pintle mount for air and close defense. The layer

The running gear of the AS 90 consists of 12 double roadwheels, six on each side and each with a hydropneumatic suspension unit. A drive sprocket is situated at the front and an idler is at the rear. The road wheels are made out of lightweight aluminum. Since a hydropneumatic suspension is used, there is no need for a false floor, which is necessary when using a torsion bar suspension. As a result, there is more headroom in the firing compartment and the howitzer has a lower silhouette. (Carl Schulze)

can traverse the turret either electrically or, in an emergency, manually. The Royal Ordnance 155mm 39-caliber gun (with its breech, recoil system and loading system) is mounted in the front of the turret between the layer and the loaders. The recoil system of the gun consists of two diametrically opposed buffers and a recuperator that together allow a maximum recoil of 800mm (31.5 inches). The AS 90 can fire a three-round burst in under 10 seconds, provide intensive fire for three minutes by firing six rounds per minute, or provide sustained fire with two rounds a minute for a longer period. Its 155mm 39-caliber barrel manufactured by Royal Ordnance Nottingham can fire all standard 155mm rounds in use within NATO.

In the British Army, the following ammunition types are available: DM 105 (Smoke), DM 106 (Illumination), L 18 (Marker), L 20 (ERBS Bomblet), L 15 (HE), L 21 (HE), M 107 (HE), M 483 (Bomblet), and XM 867 (ECM/Jammer). Using standard ammunition, a range of 24.7km (15 miles) can be achieved, which can be extended to 30km (19 miles) when assisted projectiles are used. In the future, a range of 30km will be possible with standard ammunition with the 52-caliber barrel, while the maximum range with assisted projectiles will be 40km (25 miles).

A total of 48 shells and charges are carried in the vehicle, 31 of which are stored in the magazine in the turret, while the remaining shells are stored in brackets in the fighting compartment. The magazine in the rear of the turret is divided into four compartments fitted with a motor that moves the required round into position so that it can be pulled manually onto the shell transfer arm. The shell transfer arm is now automatically realigned to lock with the elevating mass, and the shell is driven sideways onto the loading tray by a motor-driven shell clamp. After the loading tray is

Battery badge of A Battery (The Chestnut Troop) of the 1st Regiment Royal Horse Artillery seen on the battery's AS 90s. (Carl Schulze)

THE CHESTNUT TROOP

brought in line with the breach, the round is rammed by means of a flick rammer and the charge is inserted by hand before the breach is closed. Once loaded, the gun can be fired either by the layer or the commander.

Fitted with the Autonomous navigation and Gun Laying System (AGLS), the AS 90 can operate independently of external sighting references. The center of the AGLS is the ring laser gyroscope technology based Dynamic Reference Unit (DRU), which is housed by the Initial Navigation System (INS). The INS is linked to the odometer that is situated in the left sprocket, and therefore provides accurate information on the actual position of the gun. This data is combined with the information received via data communication through the VRC 351 radio of the vehicle and then transferred into the Gun Display Unit (GDU), a receiver terminal of BATES (Battle Field Artillery Target Engagement System). They automatically provide the crew with a fire commando consisting of bearing, elevation and required charge. All main turret functions are controlled by the Turret Control Computer (TCC), which can automatically lay the gun onto the required bearing and elevation to allow rapid target engagement. Mounted in the rear of the turret are an NBC protection system and an air conditioning system that enable the gun to fire under NBC conditions.

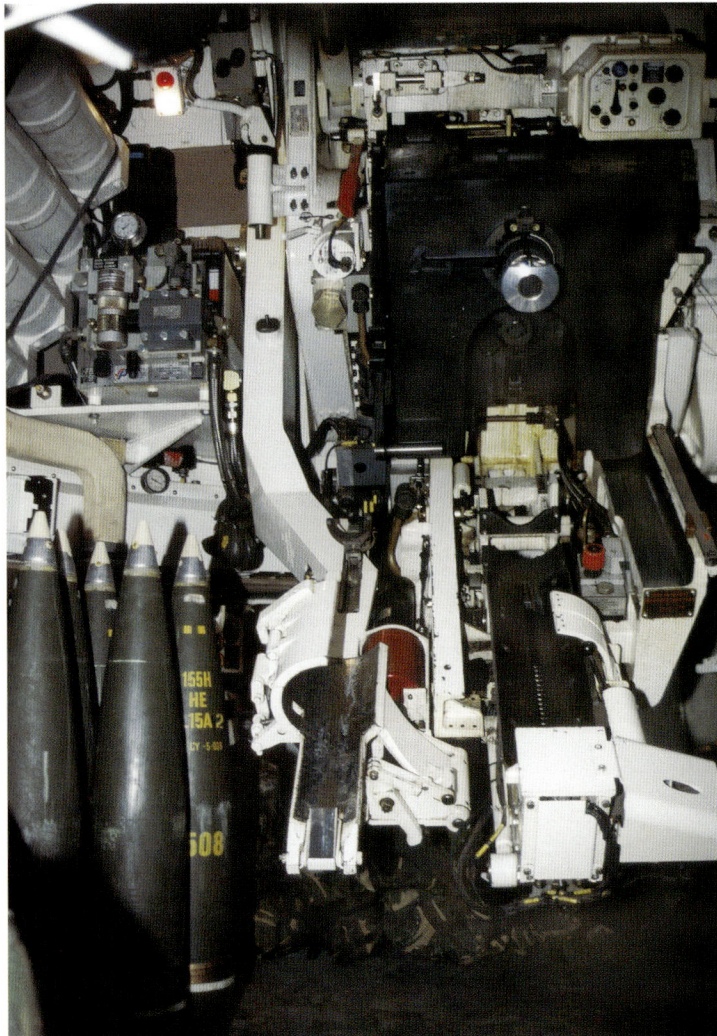

Picture of the split-block breach, loading tray and shell rammer. Together with the balancing gear, the loading tray and shell rammer are the only hydraulically operated parts in the turret. The remaining systems, like the traverse and elevation system, are electrically operated. Both can be operated at a speed of 10° a second. During fire missions, the shell transfer arm is manually loaded with a shell from the magazine and then automatically realigned to lock with the elevating mass. The shell is driven sideways by a motor-driven shell clamp on the loading tray. After the loading tray is brought into line with the breach, the round is rammed by the flick rammer and the charge is inserted by hand before the breach is closed. (Carl Schulze)

View from the fighting compartment through the crawling tunnel into the driver's position at the front left of the vehicle. The driver can enter his position via a single-piece hatch above him. The hatch can be locked open for driving in the "head out" position. When driving under hatch, the driver relies on a single periscope that can be changed into a night vision device. Usually the driver is also the 2IC (second in command) of the gun crew, with the rank of a Lance Bombardier. During fire missions he commands the gunners working outside of the gun, ensuring that the right type and correct amount of ammunition is ready. (Carl Schulze)

The AS 90 Artillery Regiments

The British Army received a total of 179 AS 90s for the price of 300 million GBP. Once the ongoing reorganization of the British Artillery has finished, 144 of these guns will be distributed among six operational artillery regiments. Three of these belong to the 1st (UK) Armoured Division in Germany, and the other three to the 3rd (UK) Division in Great Britain. The following regiments field the AS 90:

1st (UK) Armoured Division in Germany
- 3rd Regiment Royal Horse Artillery based in Hohne, belonging to 7 Armoured Brigade
- 4th Regiment Royal Artillery based in Osnabrück, belonging to 4 Armoured Brigade
- 26th Regiment Royal Artillery based in Gütersloh, belonging to 20 Armoured Brigade

3rd (UK) Division in Great Britain
- 1st Regiment Royal Horse Artillery based in Tidworth, belonging to 19th Mechanised Brigade
- 19th Regiment Royal Artillery based in Colchester, belonging to 12 Mechanised Brigade

- 40th Regiment Royal Artillery base at Topcliff, belonging to 1 Mechanised Brigade

Each of these regiments will consist of a HQ and Support Battery and three gun batteries. In peacetime, the gun batteries can field six AS 90s, while in wartime two additional guns will bring the battery's firepower to eight guns. The additional guns are kept by the regiments and are stored following proper procedures for care and preservation. Another unit fielding the AS 90 is the 14th Regiment Royal Artillery, which is based in Larkhill in Great Britain and acts as a training establishment for the Royal Artillery. In this unit, gunners from privates to officers are trained in the art of gunnery.

In addition to all other artillery systems introduced into the British Army, the unit fields twelve AS 90s for training purposes. BAE Systems RO Defence maintains another four AS 90s for further development and evolution trials, as well as for demonstrations. Included among these is the modified Desert AS 90. Of the remaining 12 AS 90s, most are used at BATUS (British Army Training Unit Suffield), while the rest are kept at a depot for war reserve.

The Future of the AS 90, Vehicle Evolution, Variants and AS 90-Based Vehicles

At the time of this writing, the British Army is the only user of the AS 90 self-propelled howitzer. In 1998, the MOD awarded BAE Systems RO Defence a contract to upgrade 96 of the 179 AS 90s delivered to the Royal Artillery with a 155mm/52-caliber Extended Range Ordnance /Modular Charge System (ERO/MCS). The first upgraded AS 90 was to go into service by 2003. The new 52-caliber barrel, which was to be fitted on at unit level, increases the effective range of the AS 90 to 40km (25 miles). The new barrel will use the existing muzzle break, fume extractor and breach mechanism. The MCS will be manufactured in South Africa by Somchem Division of Denal and contain a Bi-Modular Charge System (BMCS). The M 90 BCMS will consist of the M 91A1 low-zone and M 92A1 high-zone charges.

In 1993, the AS 90 was demonstrated at the US Army Research Laboratory at Aberdeen Proving ground using the Magnavox Howitzer Fire-Control Computer (HFCC). With the HFCC, the AS 90 was able to operate fully autonomously on the battlefield. In addition, it was demonstrated that the change from the 39-caliber barrel to the 52-caliber barrel took only 75 minutes. For export sales, BAE Systems provides a modified version of the AS 90 called the Desert AS 90. The following systems of the Desert AS 90 are improved: Engine cooling system, air conditioning system, transmission oil cooling, transmission gear range, and auxiliary power unit cooling system. In addition, a new track was fitted and solar reflecting paint and a thermal cover for the turret roof were applied.

This close up shows the primer magazine that is inserted into the split-block breach. Twelve primer rounds can be held in the magazine. The electrically initiated percussion firing system mechanism can use the standard DM191A1 or the US M 282 ingniter tubes. (Carl Schulze)

Belonging to the 26th Regiment Royal Artillery, this AS 90 was seen on the Glamoc ranges in Bosnia in February 1996. The gun barrel is in the travel configuration; the barrel clamp is situated in the front of the vehicle and provides traveling support for the barrel. The driver operates the clamp from inside the vehicle. The muzzle is covered by a canvas cover to protect the barrel from dirt and dust. (Carl Schulze)

The first live firing of AS 90 self-propelled howitzers in an operational theater took place in Bosnia on 28 February 1996 and was conducted by guns of the 26th Regiment Royal Artillery. The shots were not fired in anger, however, but to open the IFOR ranges at Glamoc. By the time of writing, the AS 90's operational deployment list includes Bosnia and Kosovo, but no shot has yet been fired on enemy positions. (Carl Schulze)

The Desert AS 90 underwent intensive trials in Dubai, Kuwait, and Saudi Arabia. However, Poland is the only nation that currently has ordered the AS 90. In 1999, BAE Systems signed a license manufacturing agreement with Huta Stalowa Wola (HSW) in Poland for the production of 72 Desert AS 90 turrets, called "Braveheart," which are due to be mounted on a locally made chassis built by OBRUM. The first two turrets were built in the UK by BAE, while the rest will be manufactured in Poland. BAE Systems RO Defence has also designed a Repair and Recovery Vehicle, as well as two different versions of an Ammunition Resupply Vehicle, based on the AS 90 chassis. None of these designs has yet reached prototype status. In addition, the Terrier FCEV (Future Combat Engineer Vehicle), which will replace the Combat Engineer Tractor of the Royal Engineers, is based on the AS 90 chassis.

These three AS 90s of B Battery, 1st Regiment Royal Horse Artillery were photographed in the summer of 1996 near Vitez. 1 RHA provided the artillery component for the British-led MND SW and, after the 26th Regiment Royal Artillery, was the second unit equipped with the AS 90, which deployed with IFOR in Bosnia. The guns were rotated through the whole area of responsibility of the MND SW in previously reconnoitered positions, which were mostly situated close to public roads in order to underline the "Show Force" policy of IFOR. Note the battery badge painted to the side of the barrel base. (Carl Schulze)

The crew enters the fighting compartment of the AS 90 through a large rear door that is also used for ammunition resupply and which may be seen open in the picture. Left and right of the door on the outside are situated two integral containers in which supplies and equipment can be stored. Seen in 1996 in Bosnia with IFOR, this gun belongs to the 26th Regiment Royal Artillery. (Carl Schulze)

Inside the AS 90 turret, the layer (No. 3) is seated to the right front, and the commander (No. 1) is located behind him. Behind the No.1 can be seen the Gun Display Unit (GDU), a receiver terminal of BATES (Battle Field Artillery Target Engagement System). The GDU automatically provides the crew with a fire command consisting of bearing, elevation and required charge. All main turret functions are controlled by the Turret Control Computer (TCC), which can be seen in front of the No. 3. (Carl Schulze)

Close-up of the insignia of B Battery, 1st Regiment Royal Horse Artillery, which was seen on the unit's AS 90s in Bosnia in 1996. (Carl Schulze)

Here an AS 90 is seen during the first live firing at the Glamoc ranges in Bosnia on 28 February 1996. The gun belongs to the 26th Regiment Royal Artillery. Behind the gun two gunners wait for orders to move spare ammunition into the gun. Usually the crew of an AS 90 consists of at least five soldiers: the driver, commander (No. 1), gun layer (No. 3), and two loaders (No. 2 and No. 4). But in operational environments there sometimes are two more loaders who carry ammunition from outside the gun into the fighting compartment. Often these men are controlled by the driver, who also is the gun's 2IC and, therefore, is responsible that the correct spare ammunition is available in adequate amounts for subsequent missions. (Carl Schulze)

In this picture the only AS 90 to be deployed with the 40th Regiment Royal Artillery during Exercise "Ulan Eagle 96" in Poland crosses an AVLB bridge. The two banks of four smoke dischargers are visible situated to the left and right of the gun in front of the turret. The track of the AS 90, which is designed by the German company Diehl, is of the double pin design. The width between the tracks is 2248mm (7.3 feet), and the AS 90 has a ground clearance of 410mm (16 inches). (Carl Schulze)

Here a gun troop of one of the batteries of the 26th Regiment Royal Artillery is seen in a "Show Force" firing position somewhere in Bosnia in early 1996. (Carl Schulze)

AS 90 of B Battery, 1st Regiment Royal Horse Artillery (1 RHA), Bosnia 1996

155mm AS 90 Self-propelled Howitzer of B Battery, 1st Regiment Royal Horse Artillery (1 RHA) in Bosnia serving with the Implementation Force (IFOR) in Summer 1996. 1 RHA was the first artillery unit to be equipped with the AS 90 gun in 1993. The vehicle is painted in the standard black and dark green camouflage pattern of the British Army. Note the Battery badge, IFOR letters and coalition forces inverted V sign.

With its elevation ranging between −89mils and 1244mils (-5° to +70), with standard ammunition the AS 90 can achieve a range of 24.7km (15 miles). Here a gun of 88 (Arracan) Battery, 4th Regiment Royal Artillery is in a firing position south of Banja Luka with SFOR in April 1997. Note that the gun position is made out of Hesco Bastion Concertainer Defence Wall pieces, which provide protection for the gun against splinters of all calibers, as well as fire from weapons up to 30mm cannons. (Carl Schulze)

This rear view of an AS 90 of the 4th Regiment Royal Artillery illustrates the lack of stabilization spades. The modern recoil and suspension system of the gun allows it to fire without stabilization spades throughout a full 360° arc. This allows the gun to switch targets without moving from its position, making the AS 90 ideally suited to provide artillery fire support in a fluid battle. The photo was taken in April 1997 south of Banja Luka when the regiment provided artillery support for MND SW of SFOR. (Carl Schulze)

On 12 June 1999, KFOR forces led by British troops entered Kosovo and restored peace in the civil war-shaken province of Yugoslavia. Among the British units were elements of the 4th Regiment Royal Artillery. Here an AS 90 from that unit takes up a position of deterrence in the Serb-dominated town of Gracanica. (Carl Schulze)

"Fire!" A battery of AS 90s engages targets during Exercise "Sheldrik Sword 2000" on the Bergen Hohne ranges in Germany. The guns can be seen in a so-called battery tight position, meaning that all guns of a battery are deployed in a close area with a minimum distance of 50 meters (55 yards) between two guns. This is the usual type of firing position of the British artillery since as it allows easy re-supply of the guns with ammunition, is easy to defend, and allows wire communication, thereby limiting radio emissions. (Carl Schulze)

One tactic used by British artillery units equipped with AS 90 self-propelled howitzers is to operate within a dispersed position. In such a position the guns of a battery operate in pairs, each pair being given an area of 1km by 1km in which the guns practice fire and maneuver. This tactic is mainly used when there is a high threat of counter battery fire; constantly moving guns spread over a square kilometer are hard for any enemy to find and destroy. (Carl Schulze)

Powered by a Cummins VTA 903T 660 diesel engine, which is connected to a ZF LSG 2000 fully automatic transmission, the AS 90 can achieve a top speed of 55km (34 mph). When traveling cross-country, twelve externally mounted hydrogas-suspension units give the vehicle a progressive rate of springing, powerful damping on every wheel station and a very smooth ride, enabling high average speeds to be maintained across bumpy terrain. (Carl Schulze)

Units equipped with the AS 90 can fire off the line of march if the situation requires it. Here an AS 90 has quickly taken up a firing position after receiving a firing order during the march of the gun battery to a new position. The sophisticated fire control system, which incorporates the Autonomous navigation and Gun Laying System (AGLS), gives the AS 90 its ability to fire from unprepared positions. The pictured gun belongs to the 26th Regiment Royal Artillery. (Carl Schulze)

Belonging to 16 Battery (Sandham's Company) of the 26th Regiment Royal Artillery, this AS 90 was photographed during Exercise "Ulan Barbara 2000" in Poland. "Ulan Barbara 2000" saw the largest AS 90 concentration of the British Army since the introduction of the weapon system. The guns of three regiments, namely 3rd Regiment Royal Horse Artillery, 4th Regiment Royal Artillery and 26th Regiment Royal Artillery, were deployed for the exercise. (Carl Schulze)

This front view of an AS 90 from the 26th Regiment Royal Artillery gives a good view of the large double-baffle muzzle brake. The AS 90's 39-caliber barrel is also fitted with a fume extractor. Note the red and blue regimental badge featuring the number "26" in a black circle. (Carl Schulze)

Battery badge of 36 (Arcot) Battery of the 40th Regiment Royal Artillery. (Carl Schulze)

Regimental badge of the 40th Regiment Royal Artillery as it appears on the regiment's AS 90s. (Carl Schulze)

Battery badge of 137 (Java) Battery of the 40th Regiment Royal Artillery seen on the battery's AS 90s. (Carl Schulze)

AS 90s of C Battery, 3rd Regiment Royal Horse Artillery are lined up ready to be moved onto a train at Drawsko Pomorski station after the completion of Exercise "Ulan Barbara 2000." Note the "C" painted on the barrel clamp. Guns of J Battery (Sidi Rezegh) can be identified by a painted "J", while D Battery's guns have a "D" painted on the barrel clamp. (Carl Schulze)

During Exercise "Ulan Eagle 2000," an AS 90 of 16 Battery (Sandham's Company) of the 26th Regiment Royal Artillery fords a river at the Drawsko Pomorski training area. The AS 90 has a fording capacity of up to 1500mm (5 feet), which means shallow rivers and streams can be crossed without the engineers having to build a bridge. (Carl Schulze)

Battery badge of 52 (Niagara) Battery, 4th Regiment Royal Artillery. (Carl Schulze)

Battery badge of 97 Battery (Lawson's Company) of the 4th Regiment Royal Artillery. (Carl Schulze)

Battery badge of 3/29 (Corunna) Battery of the 4th Regiment Royal Artillery. (Carl Schulze)

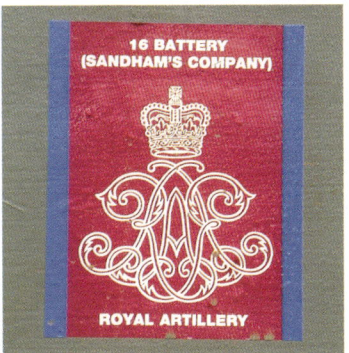

Battery badge of 16 Battery (Sandham's Company) of the 26th Regiment Royal Artillery. (Carl Schulze)

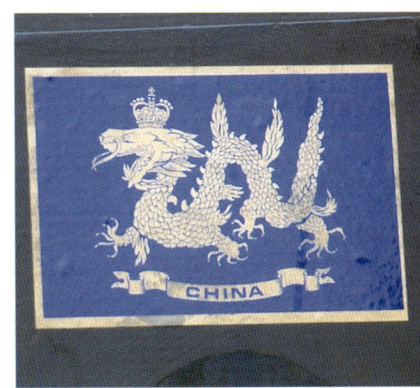

Battery badge of 127 (Dragon) Battery of the 26th Regiment Royal Artillery. (Carl Schulze)

The powerpack consisting of the Cummins VTA 903T 660 90-degree, V8, four-stroke, liquid-cooled diesel engine and the ZF LSG 2000 fully automatic transmission with four forward and two reverse gears can be changed in less than one hour. (Carl Schulze)

After the conclusion of Exercise "Ulan Barbara 2000" in Poland, AS 90s of the 1st (UK) Armoured Division approach the Drawsko Pomorski station where they will be loaded onto trains for their return trip to their bases in Germany. The "IV" on a red and blue diamond on the right side of the hull identifies the first gun as one belonging to the 4th Regiment Royal Artillery. In fact, all guns belong to the regiment's 3/29 (Corunna) Battery. (Carl Schulze)

An AS 90 of the 3rd Regiment Royal Horse Artillery changes position during Exercise "Ulan Eagle 2000." Note that the driver, commander and one of the loaders are driving in the "head out" position. The loader on the left side of the vehicle is manning the roof-mounted 7.62mm GPMG, which is used to protect the vehicle against attacking infantry and aircraft. (Carl Schulze)

After its running gear was seriously damaged during Exercise "Ulan Eagle 2000," an AS 90 of the 3rd Regiment Royal Horse Artillery is dragged to the train station with its right track missing. Towing is performed by the regiment's REME detachment, which operates a Chieftain Armoured Repair and Recovery Vehicle (ARRV). (Carl Schulze)

With a weight of 45 tons, a length of 9913mm (32.5 feet), a width of 3430mm (11 feet), and a height of 3020mm (10 feet), the AS 90 can easily be loaded and transported by rail. Here crewmembers from the 4th Regiment Royal Artillery secure their AS 90s so they will not slide on the train carriages. (Carl Schulze)

AS 90s of the 3rd Regiment Royal Horse Artillery make their way to the Drawsko Pomorski station during Exercise "Ulan Eagle 2000." Note the warning light mounted for traffic-safety purposes on the turret. (Carl Schulze)

Battery badge of 88 (Arracan) Battery of the 4th Regiment Royal Artillery. (Carl Schulze)

During an advance-to-contact operation conducted by a British armored battle group, the Challenger 2 main battle tanks and Warrior armored infantry fighting vehicles are closely followed by the guns of the supporting AS 90-equipped artillery unit. Using dispersed positions, the guns operate in pairs, one ready to fire and the other following the combat troops. This makes artillery support available at any time. Here a gun from the 3rd Regiment Royal Horse Artillery is seen during an advance-to-contact operation. The crew has just chosen a firing position and is preparing to support the leading troops with a three-round burst. (Carl Schulze)

Because artillery positions are located only a few kilometers behind the FEBA, there is a constant threat that enemy ground forces, including armored vehicles, will break through the own forces' defenses and attack the gun positions. To counter this threat, the guns of a battery, which are deployed in a tight position, have an alternative position for anti-tank purposes. In this case, the crew of the AS 90 will use the direct-fire capabilities of the gun by firing HE rounds. Using the optical day/night anti-tank sight in direct firing, targets can be engaged at a minimum range of 600m (656 yards) and up to 2000m (2186 yards). This photo shows an AS 90 of the 3rd Regiment Royal Horse Artillery that has hastily taken up an anti-tank position aiming directly at an enemy reconnaissance vehicle during Exercise "Ulan Eagle 2000." Note the open anti-tank sight visible on the elevating mass. (Carl Schulze)

After an AS 90 of 3rd Regiment Royal Horse Artillery has taken its position, four of the five crew members hastily camouflage their position. The fifth crewmember most certainly is listening to the radio in order to warn the rest of the crew in the event of a fire mission. Speed is essential in modern artillery operations because the targets usually change their positions on the battlefield quickly. In addition, enemy surveillance can rapidly locate a gun position after firing, so positions are changed after every mission. (Carl Schulze)

In August 2001, the artillery component of MNB (C) of KFOR in Kosovo was provided by the 40th Regiment Royal Artillery. Here an AS 90 of the regiment is seen at the unit's base near Podujevo. Because the KFOR deployment was a peace-support and peace-keeping mission, the gunners seldom used their AS 90s. They mainly performed patrols in the infantry role. However, the British Army also deploys eight AS 90s to Kosovo along with the gunners of a regiment. (Carl Schulze)

An AS 90 of 137 (Java) Battery of the 40th Regiment Royal Artillery at the regimental base near Podujevo during its deployment with KFOR in Kosovo in August 2001. The 40th Regiment recruits mainly in the Lowlands of Scotland, so the regiment carries the nickname "Lowland Gunners." (Carl Schulze)

Six of the seventeen rounds stored in the fighting compartment are stored in brackets on the left side next to the large rear door. Here five rounds of the L 20 ERBS Bomblet-type ammunition can be seen stored in this position. The round tubes behind the rounds are charge containers, which are situated all over in the fighting compartment to hold the charges. (Carl Schulze)

Six of the seventeen rounds stored in the fighting compartment are stored in brackets on the right side next to the large rear door. Here five rounds can be seen stored in this position. The light colored rounds are DM 106 illumination rounds, while the olive colored rounds are L 21 HE rounds. (Carl Schulze)

Here an AS 90 of the 3rd Regiment Royal Horse Artillery is recovered by a Chieftain Armoured Repair and Recovery Vehicle (ARRV) from 3 RHA Regimental REME Workshop. Clearly visible from this view is the storage basket on the rear of the turret roof of the AS 90, which is used to store camouflage equipment. (Carl Schulze)

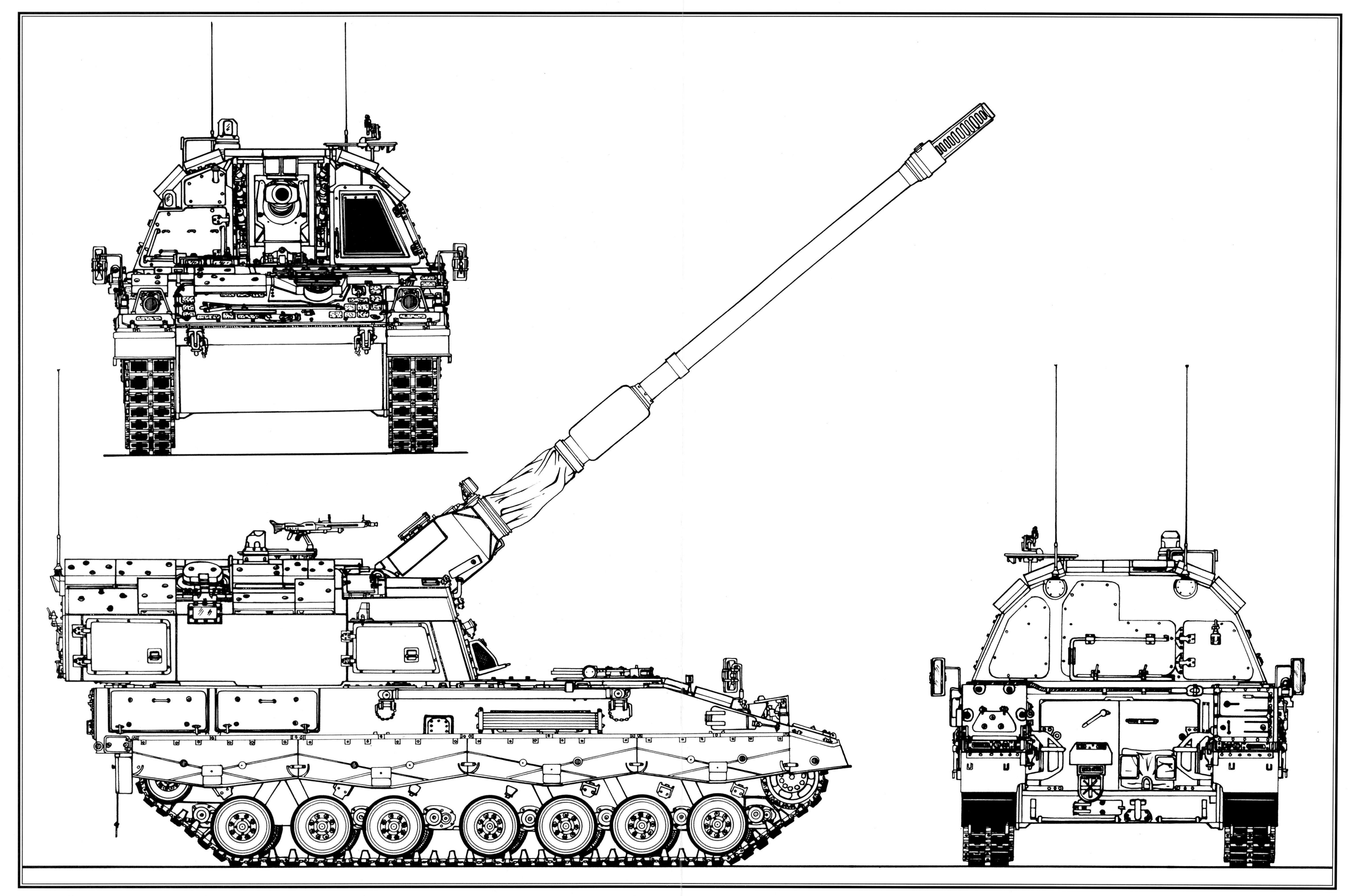

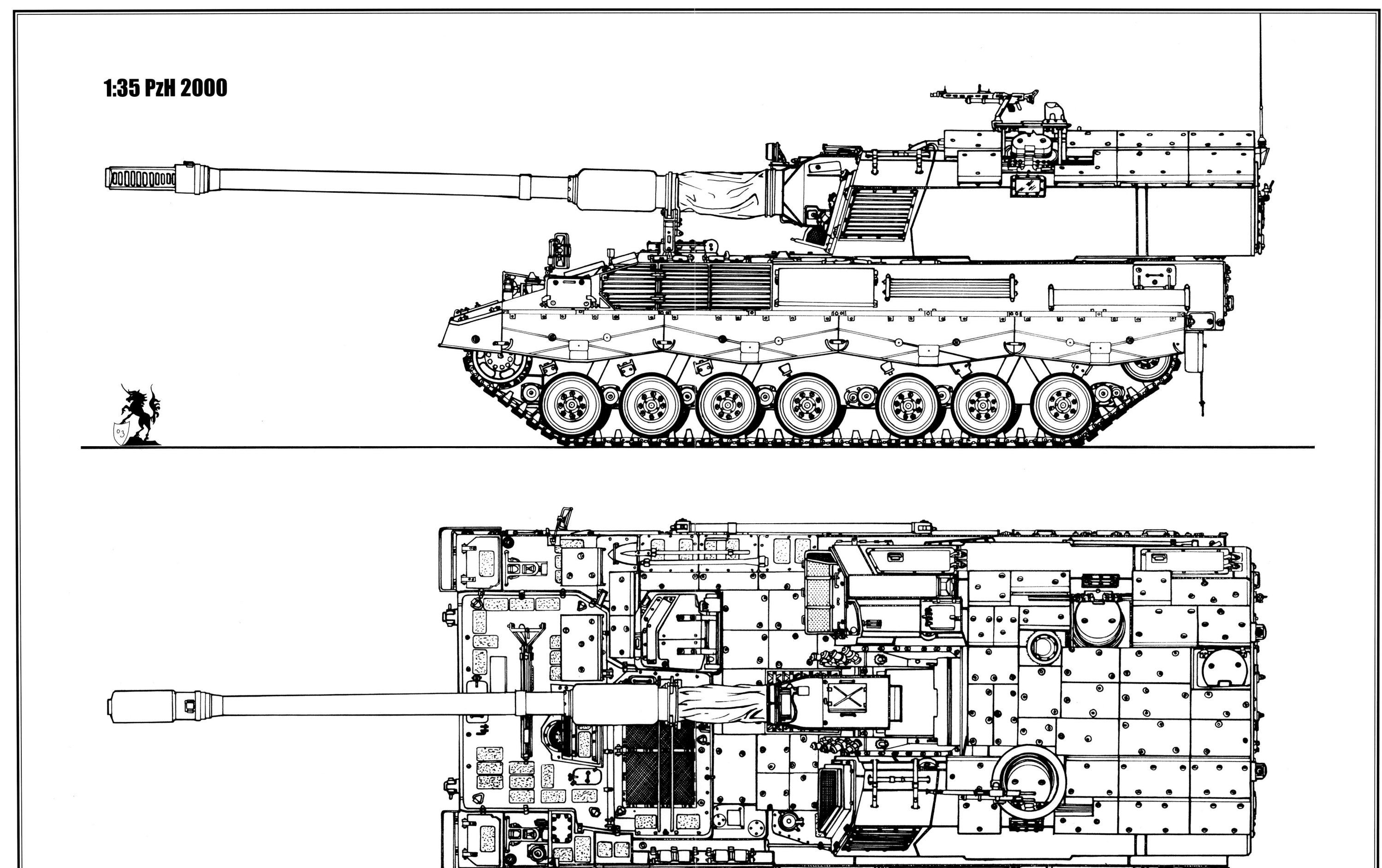

1:35 PzH 2000

M109A6 Paladin Self-propelled Howitzer

The US M109 self-propelled howitzer series is the most widely used armored artillery weapon system in the world. The M109 was originally produced by BMY, York USA. Its design and technology are based on the efforts from the 1950s. By the 1990s, the general conception of the well-proven M109 series was seen to have many shortcomings. The range of the gun, reliability, protection, firepower, NBC protection, fire rate, and fire control capabilities of the aged M109 versions became obsolete by the end of the 20th century.

In order to upgrade and update the well-proven M109 concept, in 1984 the US Army began the Howitzer Improvement Program (HIP). The aged M109 fleet variants needed to be modernized to face the threats of the modern battlefield.

Development and Introduction

In the US Army's conception, the M109 self-propelled howitzer provides fire support to the heavy divisions and cavalry regiments. To close the gap between the M109A2/A3 series and the future CRUSADER project, a wide range of modernization measures were necessary.

During the Howitzer Improvement Program (HIP), eight trial vehicles were developed: six for the US Army and two for the Israeli army. In contrast to the German PzH 2000, the M109A6 Paladin is not exactly a newly developed weapon system. The Paladin program is the third and most far-reaching improvement of the M109. Old A2 and A3 series hulls were combined with a newly designed turret. The trial vehicles, which were known by the code number "M109A3E6," were intensively tested from September 1988 to February 1989.

In 1984, the US Army began the Howitzer Improvement Program (HIP) to find a replacement for the aged M109A2/A3 self-propelled howitzer. In 1997, the two artillery battalions under order of 1st US ID, 1-7 FA and 1-6 FA, were equipped with the new M109A6 Paladin. The two battalions were restructured and ready for combat after intensive gunnery practice at the Grafenwöhr training range. (Walter Böhm)

The first troop trials were held beginning in May 1989 at Fort Sill, USA. After successful troop trials, the US Army decided to proceed with mass production. The vehicle was standardized as Self-Propelled Howitzer

M109A6 "Paladin." An initial batch of 164 M109A6 Paladin was produced until 1994. The Army also contracted for the modernization of 60 old M109 howitzers to bring them up to the M109A6 standard. By the end of 1999, the US Army ordered a total of 950 M109A6 Paladin systems and 927 M992 FAASV ammunition carriers.

By 1997, the first two artillery battalions of 1st US Infantry Division (1st US ID), named 1-7 Field Artillery (FA) and 1-6 FA, had re-equipped and restructured with the M109A6 Paladin weapon system. The units showed combat readiness during gunnery practice at Grafenwöhr training area. Later the artillery units of 1st US Armored Division (1st US AD), the 2-3 FA and the 4-27 FA, received their Paladins. Since 1999, the US National Guard units have been re-equipped with the M109A6 howitzer, as well.

Although there were some presentations and demonstrations to show off the new M109A6 Paladin, there were no foreign customers until 2002. In view of the higher firepower of the Paladin system, the US Army reduced the number of guns from 24 M109A2S down to 18 M109A6 Paladins in one artillery battalion. There are still three firing batteries, but now they only have six guns instead of eight as in the past.

Hull and Turret
Similar to the hull and turret of the well-known M113APC, those of

Old became new! The Paladin is manufactured by United Defense LP. On the production line, old hulls from vehicles of the A2 and A3 series were overhauled and upgraded, then fitted with the newly constructed turrets. By the end of 2001, United Defense LP had delivered 950 M109A6 Paladin and 927 M992A2 FAASV ammunition carriers to the US Army. (Walter Böhm)

"Mobility." The old A2 and A3 hulls were upgraded with new torsion bars, hydropneumatic suspensions and a new powerpack with 440PS, which increased their mobility and agility remarkably. (Walter Böhm)

The new Paladin turret is of totally new construction. Like the hull it is welded with aluminum plates and reinforced by armored steel plates. Shown here are the M182A1 gun mount and the support for the M117A2 periscope. (Walter Böhm)

A view of the new commander's cupola with the modified mount for the M2 Cal.50 machine gun. Between the two crewmen is the cover of the vehicle's air conditioner and the NBC cleaning system. (Walter Böhm)

The main armament of the Paladin is the M284 155mm gun, which is fitted on the M182A1 gun mount. With standard projectiles, the range of the M284 gun is up to 24 kilometers (15 miles). With Rocket Assisted Projectiles (RAP), the range is up to 30 km (19 miles). (Walter Böhm)

the M109A6 Paladin are manufactured with a welded construction of aluminum plates. Important areas are reinforced with armored steel plates.

After the fusion of FMC and BMY into the United Defense LP, the newly built Paladin turrets were produced at Letterkenny Army Depot. The aged M109 hulls were totally overhauled and modernized. As main points of the Paladin improvement program, the following components were upgraded:

Chassis – The chassis got new longer torsion bars and a hydropneumatic suspension. As a result, the vehicle has better agility and mobility in combination with the upgraded turbo-charged, 8-cylinder, 71T diesel engine with 440PS/329KW.

Fire Control System – Also upgraded was the fully automatic fire control system and the new navigation system that can find a vehicle's coordinates for automatically operated gunlaying to the targets. The Voice/Digital communications system provides better communication with the fire control center. To this end the vehicle is fitted with two AN/VRC-89 SINCGARS (Single Channel Ground and Airborne Radio System); these radios are interception safe and can also transfer digital data.

Barrel – The barrel travel lock is remotely operated from the driver's position and can be locked and unlocked within seconds while the

One of the Paladin's characteristic features is the extreme elevation of the gun, which can be adjusted up to + 75 degrees. This is a M109A6 Paladin of 2nd Bn, 3rd Field Artillery Regiment (2F3) seen near the town of Kusel, Germany during Exercise "Rolling Steel 99." (Walter Böhm)

M109A6 Paladin, 4th Battalion, 27th Field Artillery Regiment, 1st Armored Division, Kosovo 1999

M109A6 Paladin Self-propelled Howitzer of the 4th Battalion, 27th Field Artillery Regiment of the 1st Armored Division "Old Ironsides" during Operation "Joint Guardian" in Kosovo in June 1999. In Kosovo the guns were seldom used and most fire missions of the guns used illumination rounds in order to support troops on the ground. This M109A6 is painted in the standard NATO three color camouflage pattern consisting of bronze green, leather brown and tar black, introduced by the US Army in 1984.

howitzer is being driven in the firing position. The driver's sights are supported by the AN/VVS-2 night sight for night driving during deployment or attack operations. For better NBC protection of the crew and a better climate inside the crew compartment, a Micro Climate Conditioning System (MCS) has been installed. The MCS provides clean and climatized air to the crew's masks and vests.

The inside of the hull and turret is covered with Kevlar liners that offer more protection against artillery fragments and bomblet ammunition. In addition, a new 650amp alternator feeds the board computers. Also, additional stowage baskets for the crew's gear and baggage were mounted on the rear of the turret.

The most important element is the spacious turret with the M182A1

The driver's position was also redesigned. An AN/VVS-2 night vision sight can be fitted onto the driver's periscope to assist him during night driving and change-of-position missions. (Walter Böhm)

gun mount. The new M284 155mm L39 gun is based on the M185 155mm gun. The range of the Paladin's M284 gun is up to 24 kilometers (15 miles) using standard projectiles. Because of the upgrading and modernization measures, the vehicle's weight increased from 25 tons (M109A2) to 29 tons (M109A6 Paladin).

Ammunition

The M109A6 Paladin carries 37 standard 155mm projectiles, two Copperhead projectiles and 44 charges in storage racks. The Paladin has no automatic shell-loading device like the German PzH 2000, so the loaders must handle the projectiles and charges manually. The range of the M284 gun is up to 24 kilometers (15 miles) with standard projectiles and up to 30 kilometers (19 miles) with the Rocket Assisted Projectile (RAP). The firefight is largely automatic, supported by the ballistic fire control computer.

Under good conditions, the rate of fire can be increased for three minutes up to four rounds per minute; the normal rate of fire is one round per minute. The Paladin can fire a wide range of different ammunition such as HE (High Explosive), HE-VT (High Explosive, Variable Time), WP (White Phosphorous), FASCAM (Family of Scatterable Mines), Copperhead laser-guided projectiles, and the so-called "Jabberwocky" rounds that are fitted with a radio jammer.

For air defense, a .50-caliber machine gun is pintle-mounted to the front of the commander's hatch. For self-protection against hostile armored vehicles, the crew has three AT-4 anti-tank missiles in the vehicle.

Summary

The M109A6 Paladin self-propelled howitzer has the capability to fulfill the Army's requirements for the next ten years. At that time the newly designed CRUSADER Advanced Field Artillery System will replace the M109 weapon system.

The Allison Transmission XTG-411-4A offers four forward and two reverse gears. The maximum vertical obstacle height for the Paladin is 0.53 meters (21 inches). The maximum trench width is 1.83 meters (6 feet). The fording capability is up to 1.05 meters (3.5 feet) without preparation. (Ralph Zwilling)

Sign of 2nd Bn, 3rd Field Artillery Regiment "Gunners." (Walter Böhm)

The M109A6 turret is fully traversable. During fire missions, the turret should only be traversed a maximum of 30 degrees left or right from the centerline to protect the chassis against the gun's recoil. (Walter Böhm)

A Paladin platoon moves into position near Spandahlen, Germany during Exercise "Rolling Steel 99." A Paladin battalion is composed of a Headquarters/Headquarters Battery (HHB), three identical firing batteries (A, B, C Battery), and a service battery. (Walter Böhm)

The firing battery is divided into two firing platoons. Each has a firing platoon headquarters and a Fire Direction Center (FDC) based on a M577A2 Command Post vehicle, as well as three Paladin firing sections with a M109A6 and a M992A2. Pictured here is a firing section of C Battery, 2nd Bn, 3rd Field Artillery Regiment during a winter exercise in February 1999 near Schöffengrund, Giessen, Germany. (Walter Böhm)

To reduce the width of the M109A6 Paladin when operating in woodland or urban areas, its turret baskets can be folded backwards. (Walter Böhm)

Thanks to its upgraded chassis and suspension, the M109A6 Paladin no longer needs manually operated spades to stabilize the vehicle when firing. But they are still mounted at the rear of the hull for use when the hydropneumatic suspension fails or additional stabilization is necessary on swampy ground. Notice the missing left turret basket. The tactical markings on the turret identify the vehicle as belonging to 1st US ID, 1-7 FA, C Battery, 1st Platoon, 3rd Firing Section. (Walter Böhm)

"Shoot and scoot." In contrast to the German Bundeswehr's PzH 2000, the Paladin is not a completely new design; it is based on proven components. Only the tactical requirements were changed to meet the threats of a 21st century battlefield. This means that the Paladin system can operate independently and far apart, move quickly to the firing position, set coordinates and fire, and then make tracks as fast as possible. (Walter Böhm)

"1st US ID DIV ARTY." The division artillery of 1st US Infantry Division is based in Bamberg, Germany. It is made up of three field artillery battalions equipped with the M109A6 Paladin: 1-5 Field Artillery Rgt. based in Fort Riley, USA; 1-6 Field Artillery Rgt. based in Bamberg, Germany; and 1-7 Field Artillery Rgt. based in Schweinfurt, Germany. The 1-33 Field Artillery Rgt., which has one MLRS battalion, completes the 1st US ID DIV ARTY. (Ralph Zwilling)

"1st US AD DIV ARTY." The division artillery of 1st US Armored Division is based in Germany, too. It is made up of three field artillery battalions equipped with the Paladin system: 2-3 Field Artillery Rgt. based in Giessen, Germany; 4-27 Field Artillery Rgt. based in Baumholder, Germany; and 4-1 Field Artillery Rgt. based in Fort Riley, USA. The 1-94 Field Artillery Rgt.(MLRS), which is based in Baumholder, Germany, completes the 1st US AD DIV ARTY. (Walter Böhm)

The Platoon Operation Center (POC on a M577A2) distributes the fire orders and targets to the M109A6 Paladin via the SINCGARS (Single Channel Ground and Airborne Radio) AN/VIC –3(v)-6 radios. The fire order contains the kind of ammunition and fuse, as well as the message whether the crew can fire when ready or wait for a firing order from the POC. (Walter Böhm)

The fire procedure is largely automatic, supported by the vehicle's mounted ballistic fire control computer. This independent Automatic Fire Control System (AFCS) has three main components: The ballistic fire control computer, the Muzzle Velocity System (MVS), and the GPS-based navigation system (MAPS). These components check all data, set own position, and bring turret and gun barrel into the right position and elevation. (Walter Böhm)

To stabilize the heavy gun barrel during driving, the Paladin is fitted with an automatic, remote-controlled barrel travel lock. It is no longer necessary to leave the vehicle to unfasten and fold down the barrel lock. (Walter Böhm)

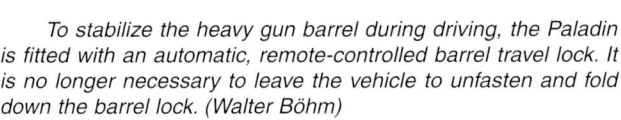

The largely automatically operated fire mission procedure makes it possible for the first round to leave the howitzer just 60 seconds after the fire data has been transferred from the POC to the Paladin howitzer. Each Paladin can operate fully independently from other howitzers. (Ralph Zwilling)

At a Forward Ammunition Point (FAP), here at Training Area at Grafenwöhr, Germany, a M109A6 is supplied with 155mm ammunition. The projectiles were transported by a HEMTT M1074 PLS truck to the FAP. The howitzers seen here belongs to the "Bull Dogs" of B Battery, 2nd Bn, 3rd Field Artillery Regiment. In the event of war or crisis, this unit is under order of 1st Ready Brigade Combat Team, 1st US AD. (Walter Böhm)

Emblem of Bravo Battery (Bull Dogs), 2nd Bn, 3rd Field Artillery Rgt. (Walter Böhm)

The M109A6 Paladin self-propelled howitzer can fire a wide range of different types of 155mm ammunition: HE (High Explosive), HE-VT (High Explosive, Variable Time), WP (White Phosphorous), projectiles with scatterable mines of the FASCAM series, and laser-guided "Copperhead" projectiles. (Walter Böhm)

To make rearming easier and faster for artillery troops, the US Army ordered the M992A2 FAASV special vehicle for supporting the M109 howitzer. To move the rounds from the M992A2 (nickname: "CAT") to the M109A6, the vehicles are positioned back to back. By means of a conveyor belt, eight rounds per minute can be transferred over to the Paladin's ammunition racks. In the US Army today, each M109A6 in the Paladin-equipped field artillery battalions are paired up with a M992A2 FAASV for ammunition transport. These two vehicles work together as the Firing Section. (Walter Böhm)

"CAT." The chassis of the M992A2 FAASV (Forward Artillery Ammunition Supply Vehicle) is largely identical to the M109A2 chassis. The turret was replaced by an armored hull based on aluminum plates. This provides protection for the crew and the ammunition against small arms fire and artillery fragments. The M992A2 FAASV can carry 93 155mm projectiles, 99 charges and 104 fuses, enough to completely rearm a M109A6 Paladin three times. (Walter Böhm)

On streets, the M109A6 Paladin can reach a speed 64km/h (40 mph). It has a range up to 351 kilometers (218 miles), depending on the terrain and conditions. After all the upgradings, the M109A6 now has a combat weight of 29 tons. The power-to-weight ratio is 15.25hp/ton. (Walter Böhm)

"First Lightning." During exercises or in case of war or crisis, the M109A6 Paladins of 1st Bn, 7th Field Artillery Rgt. support the combat units of 2nd Dagger Brigade Combat Team of 1st US ID, which is based in Schweinfurt, Germany. The 1-7 FA, nicknamed "First Lightning," was founded in 1916 during World War One and later participated in every important US Army operation up to the present. (Walter Böhm)

A Paladin from 4th Bn, 27th Field Artillery Rgt. is refueled on a forest path near Trier, Germany during Exercise "Rolling Steel 99." The Paladin has a fuel capacity of 504 liters (133 gallons) of diesel fuel. (Walter Böhm)

The deployment of Paladin artillery battalions over far distances is supported by trains of the German Bundesbahn. In 1-7 FA, it is common to paint the name of the vehicle's commander and driver on the left and right front mud flaps. (Walter Böhm)

A M109A6 Paladin of 4th Bn, 27th FA, 1st US AD crosses the Mosel River on a Ribbon bridge from the 130th Engineer Brigade during Exercise "Rolling Steel 99." The design of the Russian 2S3 self-propelled howitzer is very similar to the concept and design of the proven US M109 series. Today the Chinese company NORINCO (China North Industries Corporation) produces a detailed copy of the US M109. This Chinese howitzer can also use a wide range of standard NATO 155mm ammunition. (Walter Böhm)

The future of the US Army self-propelled howitzer is the CRUSADER Advanced Field Artillery System. Until the first CRUSADER leaves the production line, the M109A6 Paladin has enough growth potential to fulfill the Army's requirements for the next ten years. (Walter Böhm)

155mm Grand Cadence de Tir (GCT)

The development of the French 155mm *Grand Cadence de Tir* (GCT) AUF-1 self-propelled howitzer began in the late 1960s. However, the technology for the 155mm GCT AUF-1 was well advanced. The gun can be considered the first Western self-propelled howitzer to employ a working automatic loading system. It therefore requires a limited crew of only four gunners. Today, the 155mm GCT AUF-1 is combat-proven, and its manufacturer GIAT Industries just began to offer the gun with a longer barrel and sophisticated fire control electronics that will enhance the range of the gun.

Of the 273 total guns delivered to the French Army, 94 are the upgraded 155mm GCT AUF-1 T version that features a stronger auxiliary power unit and a new, more reliable automatic loading system. While the other 179 155mm GCT AUF-1 were produced between 1979 and 1988, these 94 upgraded 155mm guns were produced between 1988 and 1996. French 155mm GCT AUF-1 guns first saw operational action during the 1995 crisis in Bosnia, when a battery of guns of the *40ème Régiment d'Artillerie* took up positions on Mount Igman and fired at Serb positions around Sarajevo.

Development History

The development of the 155mm *Grand Cadence de Tir* began in 1969 with the goal of meeting the French requirements for a new self-propelled howitzer in order to replace the older 105mm AMX 13 and the 155mm Mk F3 self-propelled howitzer. Rather than concentrating on constructing a completely new vehicle, GIAT Industries simply designed an artillery turret that could be mounted on an existing main battle tank chassis. In 1972, the first GCT turret prototype was completed, and in 1973 it was shown to the public for the first time on the SATORY defense exhibition, mounted on an AMX 30 chassis. A second prototype turret was mounted on a Leopard 1 chassis for trials that same year. In 1974, ATS Roanne (today part of GIAT Industries) built six pre-production-series vehicles based on the AMX 30 chassis. After intensive trials, the 155mm GCT AUF-1 (as the gun is called in the French Army) was officially selected for service in July 1979. However, the series production had already begun in 1977, and the first production vehicles were delivered to Saudi Arabia.

Vehicle Description

Although the turret of the 155mm GCT AUF-1 self-propelled howitzer can be mounted on most main battle tank chassis, it is currently in use only on the French-made AMX 30 main battle tank chassis. The hull remained nearly identical to that of the MBT, except that the ammunition storage racks have been removed and a 28V generator has been added, along with a ventilator system that supplies the turret with fresh air. In total, the chassis is two tons lighter that that of the original AMX 30 MBT. Of the four-man crew, only the driver works in the chassis, where he is seated at the front left. He can enter and leave his position through a single-piece hatch. Three periscopes mounted in front of the hatch allow the howitzer to be driven with the hatch closed. The center periscope can be changed into a night vision device to allow for night driving. The 155mm GCT AUF-1 turret is mounted in the center of the chassis similarly to the MBT turret.

In February 1996, this 155mm GCT AUF-1 of the 40ème Régiment d'Artillerie was seen on Mount Igman in Bosnia. Clearly visible is the AMX 30 main battle tank chassis on which the 155mm GCT AUF-1 turret was mounted. This provided the French Army with a modern but cost-effective self-propelled howitzer for which the logistics, such as spare part supply and trained maintenance personnel, were already available since the AMX 30 main battle tank already served as a weapon system. GIAT Industries claims that, in addition to the AMX 30 chassis, the 155mm GCT AUF-1 turret can also be mounted on T-72, Leopard, and other MBT chassis. (Carl Schulze)

Nicknamed "Alencon," this 155mm GCT AUF-1 belongs to the 40ème Régiment d'Artillerie *and was photographed in February 1996 on Mount Igman. Together with a second gun nicknamed "Courcelles," it was this gun that silenced a Serb mortar position on 22 August 1995 at 0840 local, firing a total of six rounds. The fire was a reaction to a Serb mortar attack on a UN post manned by Egyptian peacekeepers that injured six peacekeepers and killed and wounded several civilians. In fact, this demonstration of firepower was only an overture. On 30 August NATO unleashed massive fire onto Serb positions around Sarajevo during Operation "Deliberate Force," which eventually led to the Dayton peace agreement. Again the 155mm GCT AUF-1 of the* 40ème Régiment d'Artillerie *took part in the operation, pulverizing Serb positions with accurate fire. This picture was taken in February 1996, when the eight guns deployed to Bosnia were still based on Mount Igman. (Carl Schulze)*

Here 155mm GCT AUF-1 guns of the 40ème Régiment d'Artillerie *undergo a maintenance session conducted by personnel of the regiment in February 1996 at the unit's base close to the Olympia Hotel on Mount Igman. (Carl Schulze)*

Mounted in the rear of the chassis is the Hispano-Suiza HS 110 water-cooled, supercharged, 12-cylinder, multi-fuel engine connected to a mechanical transmission with five forward and five reverse gears. The transmission incorporates a centrifugal-type automatic clutch, a gearbox and steering unit combination, the brakes, and the final drives. The tracks are powered via the rear-mounted drive sprockets. The AMX 30 chassis running gear consists of five road wheels and three return rollers, as well as a front idler and drive sprocket on each side. A torsion bar system is offered as a suspension system, and the first and last road wheel on each side is fitted with a hydraulic shock absorber. The steel track of the vehicle has 83 links and changeable rubber pads. Due to the recoil system of the 155mm GCT AUF-1 gun, no spades are needed to secure the gun in position, so no such equipment is mounted to the rear of the gun. The chassis and turret of the 155mm GCT AUF-1 self-propelled howitzer is made of all-welded steel that provides the crew with protection against small arms fire and splinters from 155mm artillery rounds.

Additional battlefield protection is provided by an NBC protection system that allows the crew to conduct fire missions under NBC conditions. Inside the turret the commander and the layer are seated to the right while the loader is placed on the left. Situated between them is the breech of the 155mm 40-caliber ordnance, while the magazine is found in the rear of the turret. The breechblock of the gun is the sliding vertical wedge type that is hermetically sealed. Mounted on the barrel is a double-baffle muzzle brake. Elevation (-4° to +66°) and turret traverse (360°) is achieved hydraulically with a speed of 10° per second. The inertial fire

The AMX 30 chassis of the 155mm GCT AUF-1 is powered by a Hispano-Suiza HS 110 water-cooled, supercharged, 12-cylinder, multi-fuel engine that is connected to a mechanical transmission with five forward and five reverse gears. The transmission incorporates a centrifugal-type automatic clutch, a gearbox and steering unit combination, the brakes, and the final drives. (Carl Schulze)

A look into the commander's position of a 155mm GCT AUF-1 belonging to the 40ème Régiment d'Artillerie. Even though the turret looks large from the outside, the space for the commander, gunner and loader is cramped; the 155mm gun, the automatic loader and the magazine holding 42 rounds and cartridge cases take up a lot of space. Here the commander enters a fire command into the gun's computerized fire control system. (Carl Schulze)

Mounted next to the hatch of the loader on the turret roof is a .50-caliber M2 HB machine gun, which is used for air defense or the protection of the gun position when it is attacked on the ground. Behind the loader, the 40-caliber barrel points in the direction of former Serb positions around Sarajevo. The photo was taken on Mount Igman in February 1996. (Carl Schulze)

control system of the 155mm GCT AUF-1 is coupled to an autonomous land navigation system that uses an optical goniometer (direction finder) mounted in the turret. Later versions of the GCT AUF-1 are fitted with CITA 20 system that consists of a land navigation system coupled with the gyroscope. For direct firing and anti-tank operations, the gun is fitted with an optical direct fire sight.

Loading is done via the automatic loader. It is possible to choose between the various types of ammunition stored in the seven racks by means of a control panel situated at the loader's position. With the automatic loader, which can be used at every elevation of the gun, up to eight rounds can be fired in a minute. However, due to the barrel heat the French Army usually fires bursts of six rounds in 45 seconds or two to three rounds a minute when the gun is operated in the sustained-fire role. In addition to automatic loading, manual loading is possible in case there is a technical problem with the automatic loading system. Situated on each side of the turret is an access door that leads to the fighting compartment. Two large hatches at the rear can be folded down to provide access to the magazine. Through this the magazine is reloaded, which holds a total of 42 rounds and cartridge cases in seven racks, each holding six rounds of the same type, and seven racks holding six cartridge cases.

The crew can reload the gun with 42 rounds in 20 to 30 minutes. It is possible to reload the magazine while the gun is firing. The 155mm GCT AUF-1 can fire all 155mm NATO standard artillery shells, including projectiles of the French Model 56/59 and American M 107 series. Ammunition types include HE, illumination, smoke, and bomblet ammunition, and base bleed ammunition is also available. Two smoke

The magazine of the 155mm GCT AUF-1 is situated in the rear of the turret. As many as 42 rounds and cartridge cases can be stored in the magazine, which is divided into seven racks, each holding six rounds of the same type, and seven racks holding six cartridge cases each. A typical combat load of the 155mm GCT AUF-1 might be 30 HE rounds, six smoke rounds and six illumination rounds. The gunner can select which type of ammunition he wants to fire on the control panel of the automatic loading system, and then the gun is loaded automatically with the right type of rounds without any other preparation. In addition, the gunner can select between a single shot and a six-round burst. (Carl Schulze)

dischargers are mounted outside the turret on the left and right sides of the gun.

The GCT Artillery Regiments of the Armée de Terre

In total, the French *Armée de Terre* (Army) received 273 155mm GCT AUF-1 self-propelled howitzers which, before the French army changed from a conscription to a volunteer force, were distributed among 12 artillery regiments. Of these twelve artillery regiments only five artillery regiments remained in the new French army structure. Today the following operational units of the French Army are equipped with the 155mm GCT AUF-1:

- 40ème *Régiment d'Artillerie* (40ème RA) belonging to the *1ére Brigade Motorisée* based in Charlons en Champagne
- 1er *Régiment d'Artillerie d' Marine* (1er RAMa) belonging to the *2ème Brigade Blindée* based in Orléans
- 68ème *Régiment d'Artillerie d'Afrique* (68ème RAA) belonging to the *3ème Brigade Motorisée* based in Limoges
- 3ème *Régiment d'Artillerie d' Marine* (3ème RAMa) belonging to the *6ème Brigade Légère Blindée* (light armored) based in Nimes
- 8ème *Régiment d'Artillerie* (8ème RA) belonging to the *7ème Brigade Blindée* based in Besancon

Each of the above artillery regiments is divided into a HQ and logistic battery (*Batterie de Commandement et Logistique*), a tactical operation center battery (*Batterie des Opérations*) and three equally structured gun batteries (*Batteries de Combat*). Each gun battery fields two gun groups of four 155mm GCT AUF-1 and two AMX 10 VOA forward observation officer vehicles. In total, a French artillery regiment equipped with the 155mm GCT AUF-1 can field 24 guns. Currently, 120 guns are operated within the French artillery regiments, with some being used at the artillery school in Draguignan. The remaining guns delivered to the French army are kept in depots as a war reserve.

Non-French GCT users, GCT Vehicle Evolution and Variants

In addition to being used by the French, the 155mm GCT AUF-1 was exported to Kuwait, Saudi Arabia and Iraq. Curiously, Saudi Arabia was the first user to receive series production vehicles in 1978. In total, GIAT Industries delivered 51 GCTs to that country. The fleet of 18 155mm GCT AUF-1s sent to Kuwait were mothballed at the time of writing. It is not known what happened to the 86 155mm GCT AUF-1s that were delivered to Iraq, but it is certain that some were lost during the 1991 Gulf War. During the Iraq-Iran War that took place between 1980 and 1988, Iraq successfully used the firepower of the 155mm GCT AUF-1 to stop several Iranian offensives.

Pictured from high ground, this 155mm GCT AUF-1 belonging to the 40ème Régiment d'Artillerie was spotted on Mount Igman in February 1996. Clearly visible is the commander's cupola, which is equipped with periscopes for all around observation, as well as the loader's cupola with its roof-mounted .50-caliber machine gun. Also visible are the driver's position with its three periscopes (the central one can be changed to a night driving device) and the open side door of the turret, a similar one of which is located on the opposite side. The white markings on the side of the turret below the name of the gun ("Alencon") show that the gun has fired rounds in action. (Carl Schulze)

"Celles" is another 155mm GCT AUF-1 of the 40ème Régiment d'Artillerie that was seen on Mount Igman in February 1996. Note the crew-made storage baskets mounted on the front of the turret. Pictures in other publications show the baskets filled with logs of wood that serve as additional protection from Serb mortar and artillery splinters. (Carl Schulze)

GCT AUF-1, *40ème Régiment d'Artillerie*, Bosnia 1996

This 155mm GCT AUF-1 belongs to 40ème Régiment d'Artillerie and was seen on Mount Igman, Bosnia in February 1996. During that time the regiment provided the French lead Multinational Division South-East (nicknamed "Salamandre") artillery support with its two batteries each with eight GCT AUF-1. One battery was based on Mount Igman and the other north to Mostar, in this way the regiment was able to support units in the whole area of responsibility of the division. This gun is called "Cellas", note the IFOR markings on the turret side.

The 155mm GCT AUF-1 turret was shown mounted on a T-72 MBT chassis by GIAT Industries at several exhibitions of defense equipment, and it took part in the 1995 competition for the new Indian Army self-propelled howitzer. India planned to use the turrets with locally manufactured T-72M1 or Arjun chassis, but a final decision was never made, and in 1998 another competition without French contribution took place. From 2002 onward, GIAT Industries will upgrade 174 155mm GCT AUF-1s of the French Army to the AUF-2 standard. Of these only 70 will receive the longer 155mm 52-caliber barrel.

The 155mm GCT AUF-2 uses the same turret hull as the AUF-1, but features a number of improvements: a 155mm 52-caliber barrel that increases the range of the gun to 42km (26 miles) with base-bleed shells and allows 10 rounds to be fired in one minute; an elevation range that is increased to +70°; Multi Round Simultaneous Impact (MRSI) capability; a modified recoil system; a new breech mechanism; a new double-baffle muzzle brake; a Thomson-CSF ATLAS computerized internal fire control system coupled to an autonomous land navigation system for greater target accuracy and higher mission speed; ammunition storage of 42 shells, 180 top charge modules and 20 bottom charge modules; a new powerpack consisting of a Renault Mack E9 diesel coupled with an ENC 200 transmission; and upgraded suspension for improved cross-country ability. Along with the upgrade package, it is expected that the French army will introduce a new modular artillery charge system also developed by GIAT Industries.

The last version of the gun, the 155mm GCT AUF-1 T, which is fitted with a land navigation system coupled with a gyroscope, allows the French artillery to conduct so-called raids d'Artillerie. During these operations a pair of two guns secretly infiltrates enemy-held territory until they reach a suitable firing position in range of their target. From there they open fire using the six-round-burst capacity of the gun, then they quickly withdraw behind their own lines before enemy counter-battery fire can have any effect. (Yves Debay)

A 155mm GCT AUF-1 T of the 3ème Régiment d'Artillerie de Marine is shown during an exercise in France. (Yves Debay)

Here French engineers ferry a 155mm GCT AUF-1 from the 1er Régiment d'Artillerie de Marine of the 2ème Brigade Blindée over a water obstacle. The ferry being used is a Pont Automoteur d'Accompagnement self-propelled bridging system. (Yves Debay)

Here a re-enforced gun crew is shown "bombing up" a 155mm GCT AUF-1. In total, 42 rounds and cartridge cases can be stored in the turret magazine. The magazine can also be reloaded while the gun is firing. The pictured gun belonged to the 2ème Régiment d'Artillerie, which by now is disbanded. Before the reorganization of the French Army, 12 artillery regiments were equipped with the 155mm GCT AUF-1. Each of these regiments fielded 20 guns that were divided among four firing batteries. (Yves Debay)

The 155mm GCT AUF-1 self-propelled howitzer consists of the AMX 30 main battle tank and the 155mm GCT turret. The name AUF-1 is the official name used for the gun in the French Army. Visible in this photo is the 155mm 40-caliber barrel on which a double-baffle muzzle brake is mounted. Fitted to the barrel is a breechblock of the vertical wedge, sliding type that is hermetically gas-sealed to prevent powder fumes from entering the crew compartment and contaminating the crew's breathing air. (Yves Debay)

This battery belonging to the 3ème Régiment d'Artillerie de Marine is on the march to a new position. The 155mm GCT AUF-1 chassis, which is basically that of the AMX 30 main battle tank, is powered by a Hispano-Suiza HS 110 water-cooled, supercharged, 12-cylinder, multi-fuel engine that develops 720hp at 2000rpm. This allows the gun to achieve a maximum road speed of 60km/h (37mph). (Yves Debay)

Based close to the Canjeurs training area in southern France, the 3ème Régiment d'Artillerie de Marine supports the French school of artillery in Draguignan. Here a 155mm GCT AUF-1 from that regiment is being guided into its firing position during a demonstration. The gun has a combat weight of 42 tons. The soldier in the foreground provides a good reference for the dimensions of the gun. The 155mm GCT AUF-1 is 10250mm (33.6 feet) long, 3115mm (12.2 feet) wide and 3250mm (10.6 feet) high. (Yves Debay)

This rear view of 155mm GCT AUF-1s from the 2ème Régiment d'Artillerie, a unit which by now is disbanded, illustrates well the two large rear hatches that allow access to the magazine located in the turret. The turret mounted on the AMX 30 chassis is a curious looking sight, but with the 155mm GCT AUF-1 the French Army fields a modern artillery system that still has some growth potential. The first step will be the fitting of a 52-caliber barrel that will increase the effective range of the gun to 40km (25 miles). (Yves Debay)

Here half of a battery of 155mm GCT AUF-1 of the French Army practices live firing at a training area somewhere in France. The 155mm GCT AUF-1 is able to fire a six-round burst in one minute. This means that a full battery of eight guns is able to deliver 48 shells, about 2 tons of steel and explosives, to an enemy target in one minute at a distance of 24km (15 miles). When the 155mm GCT AUF-1 entered service with the French Army in 1979, it was the most advanced artillery piece in the West's inventory. (GIAT Industries)